My Very Own Book of The Lord's Prayer

Rosalie Turner

Illustrated by Charles Cox

Abingdon Press
Nashville

With love and gratitude
to my family:
my husband, Frank Kile,
our sons Kile and Joel,
and in memory of our son Terry

This book is printed on acid-free paper.

Library of Congress Cataloging-in-Publication Data

Turner, Rosalie, 1941-
My very own book of Lord's prayer.
Summary: Presents the Lord's prayer and explains it phrase by phrase.
1. Lord's prayer—Juvenile literature. [1. Lord's prayer] I. Title.
BV232.T87 1986 226'.96077 85-30666

ISBN 0-687-27617-9

Manufactured in the United States of America

The Lord's Prayer

Our Father, who art in heaven, hallowed be thy name.
Thy kingdom come, thy will be done on earth as it is in heaven.
Give us this day our daily bread.
And forgive us our trespasses, as we forgive those who trespass against us.
And lead us not into temptation, but deliver us from evil.
For thine is the kingdom, and the power, and the glory, forever. Amen.

One day, the disciples asked Jesus to teach them to pray. They could tell that when Jesus prayed, he was talking to God. They could also see that talking to God helped Jesus to be a loving, strong, brave person. They wanted to be like Jesus and they wanted to talk to God the way Jesus did.

Jesus taught them a special prayer. It is now called the Lord's Prayer because it was taught to the disciples by Jesus. This story is in our Bible, Matthew 6:9-13 and Luke 11:2-4.

People in churches around the world pray the Lord's Prayer. You can learn and pray it, too!

Our Father, who

art in heaven,...

"Who art in heaven" is an old-fashioned way of saying "who is in heaven."

Jesus taught that God is like a father to us and he really cares about us. God is with us when we need him.

We can't see him the way we see other people. We think of God as if he were over us in heaven, looking on us to see when we need him.

hallowed be

thy name.

"Hallowed" means "holy" or "special." To remind us how very special God is to us, we say that even his name is holy and special.

"Thy" is the old-fashioned way of saying "your."

Thy kingdom

done on earth as

come, thy will be

it is in heaven.

God's kingdom is where God is.

God's "will" means what God wants for us, and he wants us to be as loving and kind as Jesus.

If we try to have God's kingdom on earth and to do his will, it means we will try to be the best we can be. We will try to be like Jesus.

Give us this day

our daily bread.

This tells us that everything in the world, including all we have, is part of God's creation. We thank God and praise him for everything, even our daily food.

Because the prayer says "us" and not just "give me my daily bread," it also tells us that we need to help all people in God's whole family get the food they need to live. We are God's helpers on earth.

And forgive us
as we forgive tho
against

our trespasses,

se who trespass

Some churches say "debts" and "debtors" instead of trespass. Both mean that Jesus knows we want to be forgiven when we do something wrong. He knows that God will forgive us! He also wants us to forgive other people who have hurt our feelings or done something mean to us.

That's one way of being like Jesus.

And lead us not

but deliver us

into temptation,

from evil.

Being led into temptation means wanting to do something we shouldn't do. Jesus knows this happens to all of us sometimes. He also knows that God can help us be strong so that we won't do the wrong thing.

Jesus knows there is evil or badness in the world. He tells us in this part of the prayer that we can ask God's help and use his strength to make choices that keep us away from evil.

For thine is the ki

power, and the gl

This ending tells us that it is God to whom we have been praying. God is greatest of all. God deserves our praise always.

ngdom, and the

ory, forever.

Amen.

"Amen" is a word used at the end of prayers and means "may it be so."

Now you can use the Lord's Prayer as your prayer. It is a special prayer. In these few words Jesus taught us the most important things he wanted us to learn.

Jesus wanted us to love God above everything else and to know that everything we have comes from God. God really loves us and cares what happens to us. God also wants us to be loving and caring toward others.